THE BEAR IS NOT THERE!

A book about the nervous system +
coping strategies

SARA OLSHER

mighty + bright

Did you know that every living thing is
made up of tiny little guys called cells?

Every cell has a job.
Together they build body parts, then tell them how to work.
They make hearts pump, legs walk, and lungs breathe.

We are cells! We are sooo tiny, you can't even see us. But we are what bodies are made of.

Hi! We are skin cells!

And we are heart cells!

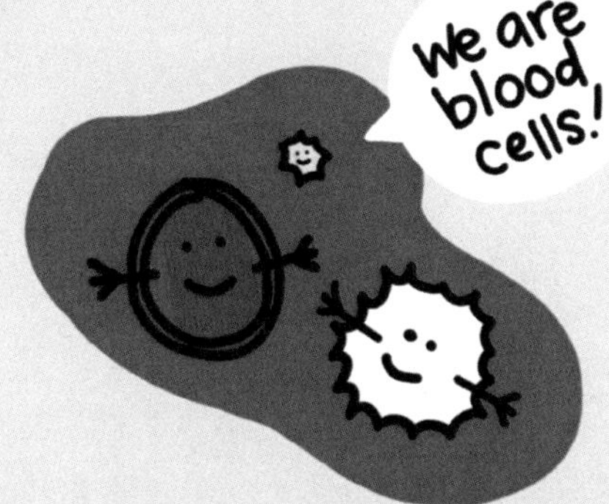
We are blood cells!

One kind of cell is called a **neuron.**

A neuron's job is to talk and send messages all around your body.

Some messages come from your brain to other parts of your body, and some messages come from the body to your brain.

Neurons line up in big strings all over your body.

When a message comes from the brain, the neurons tell
each other the message until it gets to where
it's going - like your legs or your arms.

It's like one guy passes a note to another
guy, and then another guy, until
finally it gets to the right place.

All of this happens *super* fast.

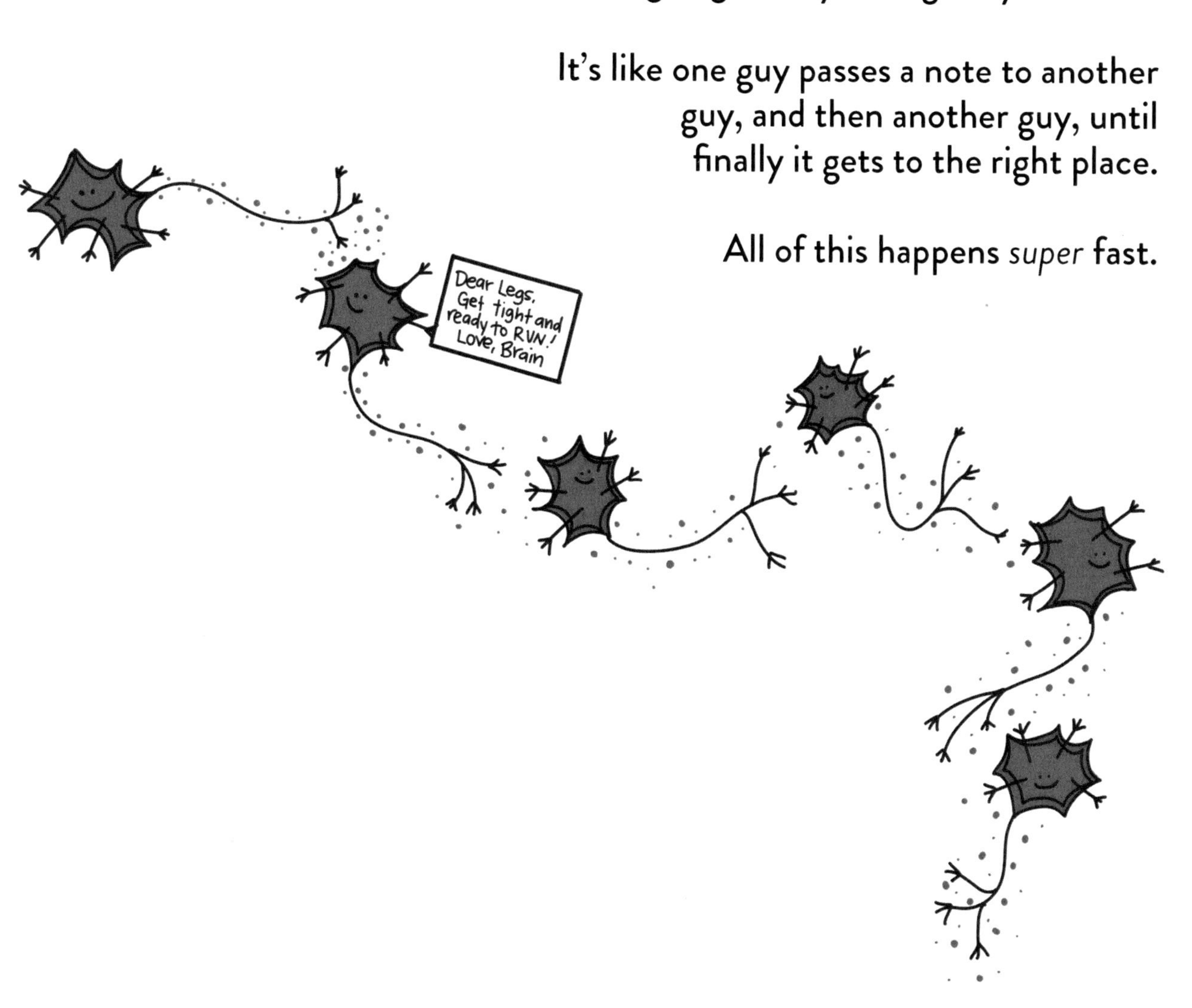

The brain decides when something is fun, and when something is dangerous.

By sending messages to your arms and legs, it can make you **STOP** when you get to the edge of a giant cliff, so you don't fall off.

It can make you **RUN** when a swarm of angry bees are chasing you.

And it can make you **FIGHT** when someone tries to take your *very special* taco.

(Most people would fight for the best taco, don't you think?)

Sometimes this is very helpful.

Like if you were going to DROP YOUR TACO OFF A CLIFF and your brain told your hand to grab it!

But other times, it is *not* very helpful.

Sometimes our brain decides something is dangerous when it actually *isn't*.

The brain yells *DANGER!!* and the neurons start sending messages *everywhere*.

All of a sudden, your body is doing all *sorts* of unhelpful things.

Let's pretend that like Mia, your brain was scared by this bear. At first, your brain thought it was a real bear.

Before you even *think a thought*, your brain is yelling ***DANGER!!*** *IT'S A BEAR!!* and is giving your body directions to save your life.

You drop this book.

You're running.

You're sweating.

You can't breathe.

You feel *scared*.

All of this over a drawing of a stuffed bear!

If it *had* been a bear, that probably would have been helpful.

But... the bear isn't there. He didn't try to hurt you.

When you realize it's not *really* a bear, you might get frustrated. You might start to cry because it is all *too much.*

Maybe you feel *angry* that you got scared about a fuzzy wuzzy teddy bear that *shouldn't even have been scary at all because it's fuzzy and wuzzy and not even a bear at all!* And now your chest is tight and your stomach hurts and you feel like *hitting* something!

Sometimes our brains make mistakes, and they mistake a sweet little fuzzy wuzzy bear drawing for a real, live, kid-eating bear.

IT'S A BEAR!

LEGS! RUN!

VOICE! SCREAM!

LUNGS, GET READY TO WORK HARD!

ARMS! RAISE UP AND LOOK BIG!

Dear Arms, I saw its teeth. Flail! Love, Brain

Dear Tummy, DANGER! Throw up now! Love, Brain

Dear Lungs, Start working extra hard! Love, Brain

Dear Legs, That is totally a bear. RUN! Love, Brain

Dear Voice, Bear = Death So SCREAM!!! Love, Brain

That's why it's really important to learn to listen to the messages your brain is sending and decide: *is there a bear there?*

Learning to do this can be *hard*.

When our bodies are sweating and it's hard to breathe and we're screaming and crying, our bodies and our brains feel *terrible*.

And sometimes we feel even *more* terrible because we start thinking big thoughts.

And then we start to feel even *worse* because it feels like we might feel that way *forever*.

If we can practice catching our emotions *before* they take control of our bodies and brains, things get a lot easier.

Did you know that we all have a hidden way to help our brains calm down?
We can get our neurons to help us!

See, it isn't just our brains that send messages to our bodies.
Our bodies can talk to our brains, too!

And our neurons can tell our brains to calm down.

That way, your body and your brain are able to see things for what they really are: fuzzy, wuzzy, and not kid-eating.

Wanna know how to do it?

OF COURSE YOU DO, because it's AWESOME.

There are *lots* of ways
to get your neurons to calm
your body and brain down,
including...

Our bodies and brains need different things at different times.
Breathing might work one time but not the next.

That's why we need to learn a *bunch* of different strategies.

name it to tame it
When we name our emotions and the feelings they make in our body, we take away their power. Emotions are like balloons that keep filling with air when you ignore them. Ignore them long enough, and they explode!
ANGRY!
SCARED
FURIOUS!
Excited!
CONFUSED
GRUMPY
UNCOMFORTABLE
SHY
depressed.
Sad

When we name our emotions and let ourselves feel the feelings in our body, they take about 90 seconds to float away.

Lots of people say "take a deep breath" when you feel a big feeling.

When you breathe in, your neurons make your heart beat faster.
When you breathe out, your neurons tell your heart to beat slower.

And when your heart beats slower, your body calms down.

The longer you breathe out,
the calmer your body gets.

deep breaths

That’s why deep, slow breaths calm your body down.
Take deep breaths into your belly and blow out slowly
like you’re blowing bubbles.

Big emotions - especially anger or anxiety -
cause your muscles to get very tense.

That's because your body is getting ready
to *run* from that bear ... even if the bear isn't there.

When you do something active,
like jumping jacks, taking a walk, or hitting a pillow,
you can calm your muscles down.

The neurons in your body then
tell your brain to calm down.

The *thoughts* we think
can send messages to the rest of our bodies,
so thinking thoughts that make us feel safe can
calm our body and brain down.

Which colors, animals, people, places, or thoughts help you feel safe?

Do you feel safe when you are alone or with someone else?

In a small space or an open space?

Indoors or outdoors?

Drawing your safe place or imagining it in your mind and describing it out loud makes your brain experience what it would be like to actually *be* in that place. Your neurons start sending messages that say "it's safe!"

Once our brains are calm,
we can think more clearly about what's going on around us.

POP QUIZ
Is this a bear?
Your pencil broke.
Your sister gives you a rude look.
Your family is out of your favorite toast.

Pretty sure none of those is a bear, even if they are annoying.

Once your brain understands there's no bear there ...
Wait... is that bear STUFFED?
I think I can stop running.
I should probably stop screaming.
Should I try to touch the bear?
Does it even make sense that it's a real bear?
Dear Arms, I saw its teeth. Flail! Love, Brain
Dear Tummy, DANGER! Throw up now! Love, Brain
Dear Lungs, Start working extra hard! Love, Brain
Dear Legs, That is totally a bear. RUN! Love, Brain
Dear Voice, Bear = Death So SCREAM!!! Love, Brain

... you can make a decision about what to do next.

Even after the brain understands there's no bear,
it takes the body awhile to calm down.

Just try to remember that nothing lasts forever,
even though big emotions sometimes *feel* like they'll never end!

And don't forget: no one is perfect. We *all* lose control sometimes.
All we can do is our best, and remember that we are good people
who are trying our hardest.

Our bodies and brains are built to protect us from all sorts of things, like dropped tacos and big bears.

With practice, you'll start to remember that we can get our neurons to send better messages — and how to send them.

And *that* can help us enjoy the pleasant emotions more, and get the *unpleasant* emotions to pass a lot faster.

Thanks, neurons!

Hi! My name is Sara. Nice to meet you!

I wrote this book (& lots of others!) because I like to draw + help people.

I live in a state Known for trees + rain, in a city nicknamed "the cherry city."

I do all my drawings on an iPad with an Apple pencil

I live with my daughter and our two cats, Waffle + Batman. One day, I want a goat, and I want to name him **CAULIFLOWER**!

Hey Parents!

You don't have to be a superhero to be an *incredible* parent.

There's no shortage of parenting information out there.
But most of us feel like we can barely make it through the day
... let alone thoughtfully develop the skills our kids need.

At Mighty + Bright, we've figured out how to:

- Incorporate emotional + mental wellbeing into your day-to-day life
- Learn a common language with your kids
- Make your parenting life easier
- Reduce meltdowns and underlying anxiety

...with no thick parenting books,
(and no digital parenting courses.)

We believe it shouldn't take *more* effort to guide your kids the way you want to guide them.
It just takes a different perspective.

Book Sara for school visits and
public speaking at saraolsher.com

Published by Mighty + Bright
mightyandbright.com

ISBN: 979-8-9851984-4-7

Made in the USA
Middletown, DE
15 November 2024

64638056R00022